Snow Leopard
Aaron Carr
AV2 WORLD LANGUAGES

Go to **openlightbox.com**, and enter the book's unique code.

BOOK CODE

R676342

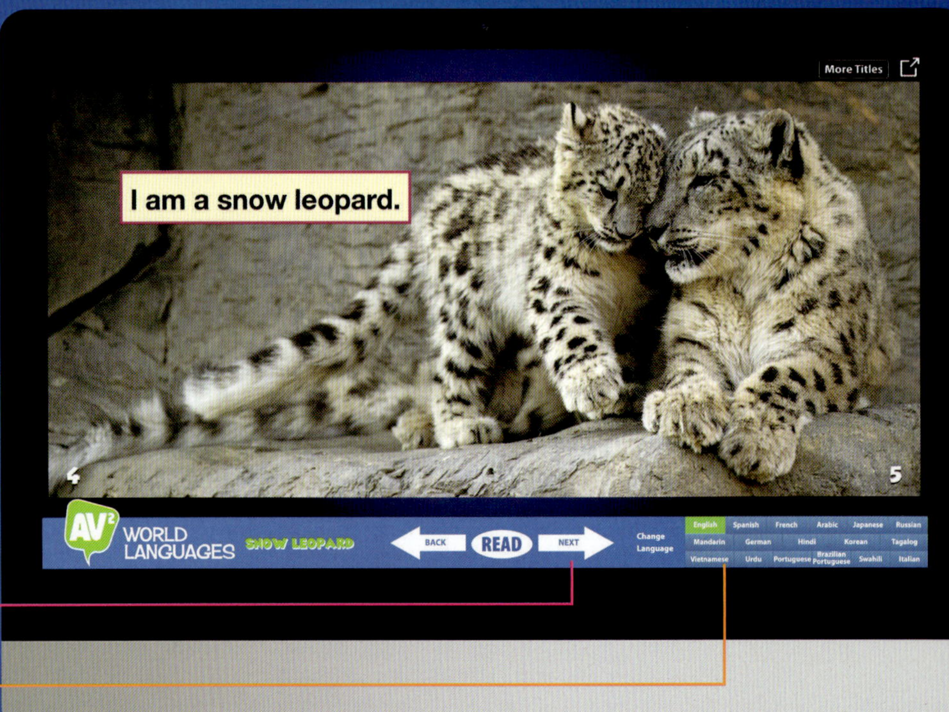

Easily move through highly visual pages.

Toggle between your **17 books in 17 languages.**

The digital components of this book are guaranteed to stay active for at least five years from the date of publication.

This title is part of our AV2 World Languages digital subscription.

Published by AV2
276 5th Avenue, Suite 704 #917
New York, NY 10001
Website: www.openlightbox.com

Library of Congress Control Number: 2017951618

ISBN 978-1-4896-6574-4 (hardcover)
ISBN 978-1-4896-6575-1 (multi-user eBook)

Printed in Guangzhou, China
2 3 4 5 6 7 8 9 0 28 27 26 25 24

062024
240614

Senior Editor: Heather Kissock Art Director: Terry Paulhus

Weigl acknowledges Getty Images and iStockphoto as the primary image suppliers for this title.

Access all of the AV2 World Languages titles with our digital subscription.

1-Year World Languages Subscription ISBN
978-1-4896-8345-8

Snow Leopard
In this book, I will teach you about
• myself
• my food
• my home
• my family
and much more!

I am a snow leopard.

I live on some of the tallest mountains in the world.

I roam an area as large as a city.

I can live on my own by the age of two.

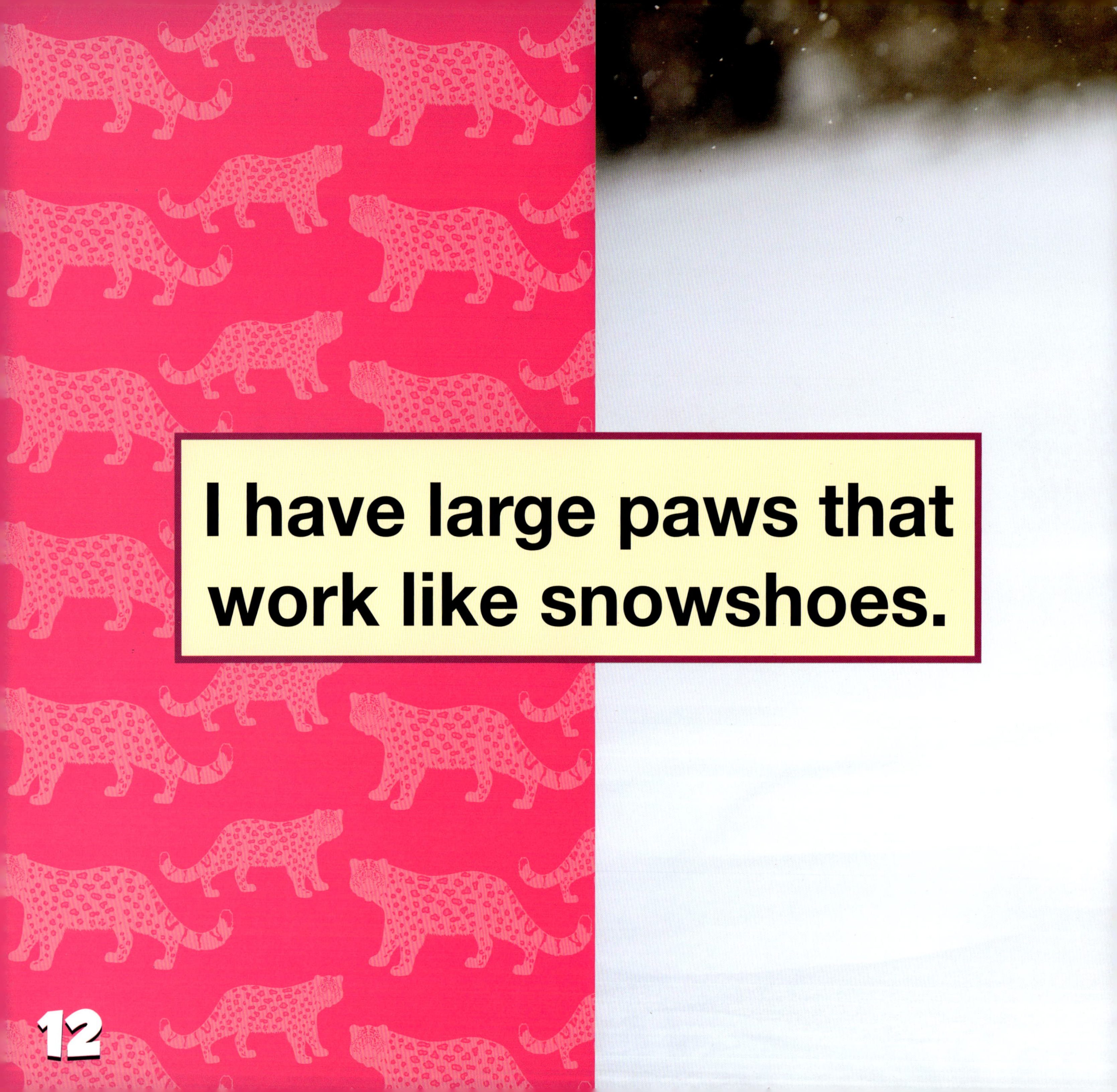

I have large paws that work like snowshoes.

I wrap my long tail around me like a blanket to stay warm.

I have fur that helps me
hide in snow and rocks.

I can jump the length of a school bus to catch food.

I live in places with few people.

I am a snow leopard.

SNOW LEOPARD FACTS

These pages provide detailed information that expands on the interesting facts found in the book. They are intended to be used by adults as a learning support to help young readers round out their knowledge of this amazing animal.

Pages 4–5

I am a snow leopard. Snow leopards are related to lions, tigers, and other members of the *Felidae* family. Snow leopards can reach sizes of 2 feet (0.6 meters) high at the shoulder and 7 feet (2.1 m) in length, including the tail. Snow leopards can weigh as much as 120 pounds (54 kilograms).

Pages 6–7

I live on some of the tallest mountains in the world. The snow leopard's range extends through the mountains of central Asia. This spans 12 countries, including China, Nepal, India, and Russia. Snow leopards prefer to stay at high altitudes, which can range from 6,000 feet (1,800 m) above sea level in winter to 18,000 feet (5,500 m) in summer.

Pages 8–9

I roam an area as large as a city. A snow leopard's home range can be more than 193 square miles (500 square kilometers). Snow leopards are solitary animals. To avoid contact with each other, snow leopards mark their ranges by scratching trees and the ground, and by rubbing their scent on rocks.

Pages 10–11

I can live on my own by the age of two. Female snow leopards may have up to four cubs, but typically have two. Cubs are born with dark fur, and they do not open their eyes for about one week. By three months, they can run and learn to hunt. Snow leopards leave their mother to live on their own after 18 to 22 months.

Pages 12–13

I have large paws that work like snowshoes. Snow leopard paws are much wider than those of other big cats. The wide paws spread the snow leopard's weight over a larger area, helping to keep it from sinking in the snow. The paws are covered in fur. This protects them from the cold.

Pages 14–15

I wrap my long tail around me like a blanket to stay warm. A snow leopard's tail can be up to 3 feet (0.9 m) long. When sleeping or resting, a snow leopard wraps its tail around its body. This protects parts of its body that are more sensitive to the cold, such as its legs and paws. The snow leopard also uses its tail for balance.

Pages 16–17

I have fur that helps me hide in snow and rocks. Snow leopards have fur made up of a thick, woolly undercoat and an outer coat of longer hairs. The fur is a mix of light gray or cream colored fur with darker spotted patterns, called rosettes, that become lighter during winter. This coloring helps snow leopards to stay camouflaged in their snowy mountain homes.

Pages 18–19

I can jump the length of a school bus to catch food. Snow leopards use camouflage and stealth to hunt. When prey comes close, a snow leopard pounces on top of the animal to capture it. The snow leopard's extremely strong legs help it to leap up to 50 feet (15 m), more than six times the length of its own body.

Pages 20–21

I live in places with few people. With a population between about 4,000 and 6,500, snow leopards are an endangered species. Humans are increasingly moving into snow leopard habitats. With a habitat range that is constantly shrinking, snow leopards have turned to hunting domestic animals for food. People are now hunting snow leopards to protect their animals.

KEY WORDS

Research has shown that as much as 65 percent of all written material published in English is made up of 300 words. These 300 words cannot be taught using pictures or learned by sounding them out. They must be recognized by sight. This book contains 36 common sight words to help young readers improve their reading fluency and comprehension. This book also teaches young readers several important content words, such as proper nouns. These words are paired with pictures to aid in learning and improve understanding.

Page	Sight Words First Appearance
4	a, am, I
6	in, live, mountains, of, on, some, the, world
8	an, as, city, large
10	by, can, my, own, two
12	have, like, that, work
14	around, long, me, to
16	and, helps
18	food, school
20	few, people, places, with

Page	Content Words First Appearance
4	snow leopard
8	area
12	paws, snowshoes
14	blanket, tail
16	fur, rocks, snow
18	bus, length